Requiem for Ernst Jandl

THE
SEAGULL
LIBRARY OF
GERMAN
LITERATURE

Requiem for Ernst Jandl

Friederike Mayröcker

TRANSLATED BY ROSLYN THEOBALD

LONDON NEW YORK CALCUTTA

This publication has been supported by a grant from
the Goethe-Institut India

Seagull Books, 2022

Published as part of the Seagull Library of German Literature, 2022

ISBN 978 1 8030 9 042 9

British Library Cataloguing-in-Publication Data
A catalogue record for this book is available from the British Library.

Typeset by Seagull Books, Calcutta, India
Printed and bound by WordsWorth India, New Delhi, India

Requiem for Ernst Jandl

Paraphrase on 1 Poem
by Ernst Jandl

('in the kitchen it is cold
winter has an awful hold
mother's left her stove of course
and I shiver like a horse' EJ)

in the kitchen we're now standing
stirring spoon in empty pot
at the window we're now standing
in this mind 1 poem we've got

6 June 2000

'and no longer linger here'

Requiem for Ernst Jandl

'this time he's gone too far', Adolf Muschg.
'But he always comes back, you can be sure
of that, and he's as demanding as ever.' Yet
wind calmer than yesterday the way the cold
is fading and on the periphery of this cold the
wind calmer, I mean *it must be the less exact*,
etc.
In a deluge of Ludmilla rain .. when I had
already 1 x stepped into the night, had
already stepped into this night many times, in
my mind had rehearsed it for years, I had
seen him, lifeless in 1 corner of his room,
lying there on his bed, had tiptoed up to his

bed listening for him to take a breath. When
your soul is bleeding, says Elke Erb, how can
you not find words, says Elke Erb, among
Mongolia melancholy monochrome and green
passers-by, is he not sending you a profusion
of loving souls and you in their midst, I mean
you in a half circle, holding your hands, says
Elke Erb, but there is nothing like him!, I say,
the secret words, our secret words, I say.
Beginning in complete ENDLESSNESS, Elke
Erb says, you will have to begin in complete
and utter ENDLESSNESS, you are an
ORPHAN now, that is how he sees you now,
bee-keeper wise .. oh to hike up a
mountain trail again, says Elke Erb, saw that
you had already stepped into the night, and
that it had no effect : how will I get this whole
thing *bewitched onto you*, says Elke Erb,
death is bitter, death is wretched, many
calumnies are death, death obliterates and
devastates, you will have to learn how to read
again, right, not only learn to live, learn to

read, this mysterious being able to read, in such a way that the line you've just read doesn't simply fade away in a daydream, I mean this trash full of tracks, in this utterly brilliant setting of thoroughly penetrating attentiveness. And the chords barely moving, the branches bleed, while 1 blackbird *screeching* .. I saw, I heard the song of a bird DIE AWAY in an INDIFFERENT bush, because I no longer had eyes for it, nothing but INDIFFERENT bushes and branches and shrubs and an INDIFFERENT opening of mouths the passers-by and the INDIFFERENT words of friends and the INDIFFERENT chirping of this world overflowing with abundance—nothing of IMPORT, had neither eyes nor ears for thing and word and image and bouquet and book and blossom, and then the embarrassment others felt, the ones who want to comfort you, and to them I say *I've got 1 song but of itinerant foot.*
Then the branches moving and the donkey 1

donkey its mournful cry, my hand scratching
behind its ear. Floating gliding through the air
so many planes in the skylight : he always
looked up that way and counted the airplanes
the way they always criss-crossed the
heavens of our skylight .. *and oh me a lout oh
me a lout* throw my tea kettle down on the
table and scream NO NO! (1 gasp of air
wafting through a grove), someone on the
telephone tells me, just think, I wafted
through a stand of privet, I plunged through a
stand of privet, and the fragrance there was
different, likely Merano. The air of Merano,
the fragrance of a privet hedge, just think.
Is that his libido or my libido and the
Creole steps into his sleep / into his sleep in her
nakedness and he himself in his undershirt—
and I didn't want to ask what had happened as she
was about to leave, with 2 cuts / scratches in
her dark skin, 1 *gash* on her dark cheek, etc., or
he said WHEN ARE WE GOING TO MAKE 1
HOLE IN THE SKY?, she said to me : 1

intimate relationship 1 intimate relationship with
him and I wrapped my lips I wrapped damp
towels over my lips I closed my lips held them
shut with my hands, because I wanted to ask 1
more question : what were you talking about,
what did he say to you, what did I miss,
mishear, what did he keep from me what did he
keep to himself .. slid into the *Coin Rose*,
staggered, sailed into the milk bowl glided,
teared, and everything melted away, wasted.
The loss, he says, the loss of someone so
close, the loss of a HAND and HEART
PARTNER is something so completely and
utterly devastating, yet it may be, we may be
able to keep right on speaking with this HEART and
LOVE PARTNER continue conversing and may
even expect a response from this person. One
who was once of such a tempestuous aura.
Now stammered heavened, and worldwide.
Oh, and thinking you'll have turned the pages of
my calendar, how thoughtful, etc. And I'll get
home, I say, and you won't be there, I say, and

I'll go into your room and touch your pillow and
look at your shoes on the shelves and your
clothes and your baseball cap, glasses and
Swiss army knife. Francis Bacon in the
extreme, the lemon-yellow, the completely
extinguished brimstone butterfly, *the lemon
trap*, the lemon drink, the lemon-coloured
knotted-up bundle of muscles and limbs,
joints, he is smiling in the colours of
1 poster, the illustrious happenings.
Something with a lake inundated in streams of
rain, likely rain dwelling of tears .. he grasped
my hand / *these 1 thousand miles and mice*,
beyond the seas (Merano) and Merano again,
should we go again should we go there again,
he asks. Merano or Grado, he says, *the train
stations there bring tears to your eyes* / grainy
enlargements of black-and-white photographs
he took at a photo stand in the train station.
When someone asks him HOW ARE YOU, he
says : *not so good : immobile but doesn't really
matter*. I am the ONE GROWING I am the

ONE HAVING GROWN, somehow it snowed or it rained, it's early July.

It is the beach, the embrace, it's much the same with the violet-blue pond this small patch of botanic, I believe twig and flesh, *and that you wish to embrace an old coat that is about to take leave.* Voice painting it over his voice painting it over .. you my sweet corpuscle you my poor wild and sweet corpuscle and that the huge masses of blood in your soul flowing away are : so torrential : so wondrous. So torrentially wondrous with PRIVET HAIR—oh you should go down to the river, says the voice on the telephone, it would ease your pain, says the voice, the waters will transport it, I mean the waters will carry it away, you should go down the river sit on the bank and let your pain flow away, these gentle undulations, you see, these gentle undulations will carry it off, ripple by ripple .. yes, I say, then, that river flowing through a small town, at times torrentially enchanting, we stood leaning up against the

❖

railing, leaning over the railing, or sitting on a
bench behind it, arms propping up our heads in
our hands looking at the water, etc., I mean
meandering and holding hands. I am torrential
that I am so torrential as this river and simply
letting myself sail away, letting myself drift, with
the currents and *blackthorn coloured*, the silence
the gurgling silence, and we sat on the bank
holding hands .. people do things like that, and
tell stories about the boat turned around and
parked in the sand, and you lay the oars inside
before you hide it away, etc.

When you came in, he says, the light was
blindingly bright, he says, I saw, quietly, on
tiptoes, a small girl dressed in white leaving the
waste cubicle. Oh stuff of the stars, to the
tenors of Puccini's *Madama Butterfly* and we are
sitting across from each other in a cafe, like an
evergreen branch his hand on our table his
gasps of breath at the edge of the table—tears
I spilt a trail of love along our way, dripped
away shed our life's time, and suddenly I wake

up out of pale dreams I see him glowing in front
of me : we are still alive we are still speaking to
each other we are still looking into each other's
eyes, we are still here, and still quiet, soothingly
quiet, each occupied with thoughts, difficulties,
curiosity and confusions of our own, I mean the
DARTING of this silence, hills of nightingales
inside my skull *as sobbing*, what a pond this 1 is
and drops and herds, UNWATERED sweetest
of eyes, *and crutchingly Moscow, half asleep*,
didn't really speak just blathered on hurriedly.
He says : *for you we would like to .. poetical
wishes ..* quietly quietly so as not to wake him
and this is the way my handwriting is, at his
burial had the feeling I should dig him out,
Gladis called from the desert, he says,
blossoms everywhere eyeing the sun into the
window, from the east, the south and obliquely
beyond compare.
Deformation has taken place, Samuel Beckett,
hard and dangerous, we are not only more
weary because of yesterday, we are different,

no longer what we were before the fate which
was yesterday. No WRETCHEDNESS like this
1 no other WRETCHEDNESS like this 1, I
scream, throw the tea kettle down on the table,
scream NO NO, *he was completely beige, he
was completely beige*.
Throwing myself into an *unkempt* nightgown,
wild solace, crying my eyes out in his night
clothes, on his bed, etc.
This small tooth perhaps 1 like this, with his
small tooth perhaps, and his head is resting
slightly turned to the left, perhaps a small tooth
like this 1 : biting into his upper lip, while he,
already lifeless, under a shroud, *his austere
cranium, his whispering genius*, his DIGNITY
into the catheter and it sounded like crumpling
paper, instead of blood, white spilling out of his
finger. *Il pleut il pleut*—much NOEL long ago
consumed, he was torn away from me, we
might still have listened to the
THERMOPYLAE, oh son of the road, the
passionate delight of quotation, I say, Mario

writes : we are all subject to this drive to
immerse ourselves in a creative process
everyday, a drive which at the moment of birth
begins to wane, dies, making place for another
and new position in the endless moment, and
we are either made mad or blessed. Breaking
through bursting through this style, etc.
Oh and making a wilderness of the bathroom, I
say, GLADIS TELEPHONED FROM THE
DESERT, never touched your hand again,
your hand your mouth your eyes, a bit
consecrated, a bit pursed the lip the upper lip
and his head very slightly left turned very
slightly to the left, lifeless under the linen, *and
no longer linger here*, no longer want to live no
longer want to read, no longer linger here, open
up, hearing you with that powerful voice
HELLO! HELLO!, and my voice, comforting
you your fear that a stranger has broken in.
Into our midst like a saint in the darkness and
MERCY'S OBLIVION, full of Spanish, French
backpacks, *a Sunday of the sort you find in a*

mirror, had A. testing his sinuses in the
restaurant garden, a metronome, said A.,
ticking like a metronome, *singular that head on
that day*, *etc*. Now know language only when it
is recited in front of me, but nothing on my own,
it has come to this, and I stand here with one
foot in the grave : Johann Sebastian Bach. All
this talking this gasping such agitation, there is
1 dog in our midst or scruff of dog's neck, a
broom, what do I know, with broom and
bouquet and brush, I mean with my broom
swept the light out through the window, it has
come to this, with me, with us, me growing
thinner, and next, among the wilting maple
leaves, now in the middle of summer strewn
over the asphalt streets, footprints on my face
and body, *uccelli uccellini*, the little birds,
l'intelligenzia della mano : the fences the
horses : has my hand my arm got shorter now? :
1 arm 1 hand always was shorter than
the other arm the other hand, which means that
I will have to keep tugging on my sleeve in
order to cover my wrist, has my hand got so

short that it can no longer be freed, says the
Lord, I drape the heavens with darkness,
says the Lord and turning his ceiling into
sackcloth, me hopping around inside my sack O
Lord, I scream, sewn into my sack, no comfort
no word or forgiveness.

You rush almost completely mad, and bouquet
after bouquet, O Lord Jesus what would we say
to each other now, so many days after his
goodbye, and our conversations, would we
keep silent, what would he say, what would he
entrust to me, his word, his sigh or powerful
with numerous voices, he would I assume
speak with numerous voices with many voices
with assorted (unnumbered) choirs to me, there is no
escape from these hours from these days, O Lord
Jesus, I've got to go to the bathroom, utterly
destructive utterly final : THREW HAIR DRYER
INTO THE BATHTUB! AND OVER! I've got to
head for the wasteland, *Gladis called from
the desert*, he was fully wooded, someone
whispered prompted us in our conversation, I
was wearing this pork-pie hat when he came to

me in my dreams, *these somnambulant*
experiences of a shoreline society, the room of
air it was cold the room of air where we sat on
wooden benches that had no back.
I addressed you with a formal You in my
dreams, I said MAYBE ONLY A LULL, that's
what I said to him, just think, I threw the
comforter over a flower pot because nothing
MATTERED to me, happened to turn on the
radio and caught your voice, such tiny pearls
on his face on his body, and me somehow
bellowed, my days *bellowed*, later a
wilted fig leaf on the stairs. The feeling that
we're sitting in a *plaid forest*, but then this piece
of forest mixed with another piece of forest
where we had once stayed.
Oh how long his fingernails must have grown
by now, or discoloured, or fallen off, how pale his
hands, how long his hair. His upper lip *sewn*
together a bit sewn together *desiring* sewn
together, under his shroud, this small tooth
small tooth as he lay lifeless under linen, this

small tooth this small tooth the upper lip slightly
drawn in very slightly, head turned to the left,
entirely ENCASED now, as if sleeping, his
icy-chilled shirt.
Such love shade, instead of sweet Easter
bread he spit up Father Son and Holy Ghost,
ate up Son and Holy Ghost and left Father
behind on the dinner plate. Such restraint, oh,
no, he says, *we're too old for that*, etc. Digs
his flute out, starts to play.
When the time does come, which cell-phone
number shall I use, he says.
Actually inner language is the only language I
have.
1/3, 95 kilo. Upstairs, write this down on a
piece of notepaper and put it next to his bed.
Things he lived to see / things he did not live to
see.
Pecking in upper lip : pecking small tooth
.. that was the small cloud on which I am
working, he whispers.

July 2000

On : *in the kitchen it is cold*

a winter pocm / a poem of last days / a

poem you shed tears over / a po-

em / you want to put your arms around it, because it

conveys all the despair, all the sorrow, all the godfor-

sakenness of this world.

Reality backdrop : it is winter, winter '88.

I am standing in the unheated unheatable

northerly kitchen in Ernst Jandl's apartment.

We had been rummaging through the drawers of his

small desk, jammed full of notes, overflowing, searching

for manuscripts ('matter') that might in some way be

included in 'idylls' his new volume of poetry / accumulat-

ing bibliography / here in these drawers

piles of notes, handwritten manuscripts, fragments, half-

finished work, a few lines, often only one word,

written down at night or late in the afternoon,
sometimes illegible even to the author himself,
fragments that could no longer be linked with
any other work. Thoughtlessly, carelessly,
the pages pile up here, dropped in utter
and complete self-contempt, self-torment,
indifference. Page after page, the drawers
refuse any further incorporation, in the past,
a few years ago, each and every com-
pleted poem filed away in a folder, now,
to their writer they are nothing but refuse,
best buried somewhere. I retrieve one
page after the other, everything handwritten,
mostly in pencil, dashed off, beginning line
of a poem, and then finished poems,
in numerous versions, all typed. After-
noon after afternoon, actually the entire
winter of '88, we are absorbed in
viewing, approving, conserving what
has been written down. And then, suddenly,
one day, I come across four lines
dashed off in pencil :

in the kitchen it is cold
winter has an awful hold
mother's left her stove of course
and i shiver like a horse

vaguely remember : the last line must have
been a little different, there must have been
an earlier version.
The last line, which informs of the most
profound abandonment, aloneness, exclu-
sion, seeking solace in an attempt
to identify with that mute creature—a carri-
age horse in winter's cold depths, standing
in one place for hours, head hanging, in no
one's care, waiting for a human to get it
going—is so poignant.
The earlier version of the last line escapes
me, as it did Ernst Jandl, it's unlikely that it
will ever be found.
We sit down at a small coffee table, across
from each other, this sheet of paper in hand,
and ponder how the last line might be
formulated more precisely, and then Ernst

Jandl comes up with the final version as above.——My 85-year-old mother cooks every day for herself and her 66-year-old daughter, me, a noonday meal, in her cold kitchen. When I arrive around two, I can see that she is having some difficulty staying on her feet, she is leaning up against the stove. Every day when I see her like this I am reminded of the lines : mother is not at her stove .. and this day will come, possibly in the not-too-distant future. And she will no longer be standing at her stove, suddenly she will no longer be there, she will be lying, stretched out, flat, with her pale hands folded across her chest, in a place where I will no longer see her, a place where she will no longer see me, a place where I cannot reach her and she cannot reach me. This line : mother is not at her stove : conveys the damnable utterly graceless transience and finiteness of this life, mother is not at her stove—where did she go. Until

her final moment, she always fulfilled her
responsibilities, she always did what she was
meant to do.

Stove : yes, this tiny cannon of an oven with
which she nurtured us through the bitterest
of wartime winters and which if only for a few
brief hours at a time gave us all warmth, she
cooked our unremarkable meals, bread
soup, most likely, and *hamstered* potatoes.

This poem, a small masterpiece by a poet
very dear to me, was written during a severe
bout of depression and is among my
favourites.

December 1990

Murmuring Buttons, and Lake Atter

this slope down to the lake Rosenhalde on the Lake :
(not 1 single rosebush / still :
    Rosenhalde on the Lake!)
a little uphill and dull, the sun the
    sky just over the shoreline
sparkles and glitters the water *how it*
    washes up (mows)
and sailboats in your hand, I mean
    holding onto your hand dazzling
hand and eye, the freshly set table at the inn,
    I think : fingerless roofed
in too shady our midday table, etc., wanted
all of a sudden wanted to rip off to bite off a small corner

of the handkerchief
I was drying your forehead drying the
     sweat which the effort
of walking—
upstairs the house strangely enough POTTERY
     a POTTER'S STUDIO I believe
apparently the roses there the knife
     the plate both

cups / we had to ask for every single thing
     you see, the
stairs disappeared into the sand of the courtyard
     (vampire?)
the child of the foreign housekeeper
     a little, well
I don't know, I tried to be friendly
but the child just stood there like a cloud, I no longer see
     clearly, only vague contours
utterly heart-rending, why? mystery
     of this

❧

summer, I cry, gone the shimmer
   now darkening
image in my mind

for Ernst Jandl   *11–14 October 2000*

or Vermont, to Ernst Jandl

let the blessing in : the tears on the windowpanc
the quietly applauding drops on knife
    and tin
crockery and cuckolding, blessedly, and
    blessed
day. Finally drowned IMMERSED the sun
    in the glorious
sea of the tumbling heavens, in the
    streams of opened
clouds .. *and I am to go out no clothing no shoe*
and be soaked through in this
    HOLY WATER
tenderly tapping and touching instead of

the one I love : the one I lost appears, aban-
doned I am buried, rotting scaffold
    my body—
tip and tongue from beyond :
you no longer visible never visible again

3 / 4 October 2000

'the days of wine and roses', *for Ernst Jandl*

that it's a heart it's a home, some kind of dom-
cile, I tell Leo N., so unassumingly longing, I
say to Leo N., a feeling a longing to visit
you, I say, my heart aches I took his boxer
shorts out, I tell Leo N., and I pulled them on,
my mother wore my dead father's watch and
his signet ring until her own death, I tell Leo
N., always at least 1 egg in your composition
cottage, hard-boiled egg on hand, and 2 or 3 x
kiwis as well, etc., I tell Leo N., you really don't
have to make any special arrangements for
my visit, I'd really like to see you and Erna, I
tell Leo N., *from the stags praise the Lord*, and
I don't know how, how it seems how it snows

how the white rose can possibly snow this July
and this August, I mean this utterly snow-
covered July, I tell Leo N., a giant green
grasshopper visited me last night before the
thunderstorm broke out, something of wisdom
or whiteness or marzipan in the corner of 1
eye when I close my eye to apply my make-up
or I tell him YOU'VE GOT SOMETHING
WHITE IN YOUR EYE, and then he, he takes
out this *sackcloth*, just think, I tell Leo N., with
this snow-white *sackcloth*, he always had it
with him, he *wiped* his eye and kept asking,
DID I GET IT, DID I GET IT, and I answered,
YES, IT'S FINE, EVERYTHING'S FINE, even
if he hadn't got it all, etc., or the way I
thinking nothing feeling nothing on the platform /
balcony of the house of doctors I mean the
way a writer of ample proportions
approached us on a country road in her
flowered smock with open arms, inviting us
into her house, I tell Leo N., for a bite to eat,
through a stand of trees, down a forested

path, and on the way back home a few hours
later a distant relative of his, I tell Leo N.,
came up to us in an encounter that was
actually more unsettling than pleasant, and
later I asked him, WHAT'S ON YOUR MIND
AT THIS MOMENT, and he said NOTHING,
ACTUALLY THERE'S NOTHING ON MY
MIND RIGHT NOW, NOTHING AT ALL, at
another locale, she, the mother-in-law, his
mother-in-law, I tell Leo N., she was the blue
apron I mean : blue blossom in the garden,
in the branches, we walked by every morning
and waved to her, visited her but didn't, and
now I've *enthused through* all acquired
books, felt myself repulsed, I say, on 9th June,
I tell Leo N., he says : lost
consciousness, gave up on myself, and they
attached this tubing to me, I called for you,
possibly voiceless, you weren't there or
didn't come, I was utterly alone .. you are my
everything, on 8 January '98 as a
dedication written down in the Critical

Edition, I tell Leo N., as first I thought it was
shards of broken glass on the kitchen floor
but it was spilt milk, little puddles of spilt milk,
that is, slugs, an oath, the spilt milk on the
burner formed a heart, *yes*, he said, I tell Leo
N., *1 heart can break that is 1 anatomy*.
And what about the pencil, I say to B., why
on the morning of his death did he draw a
pencil on a piece of note paper, I say to B.,
why did he ask for a pencil, there were
plenty of pens on the little table next to his
bed, the quill of the Holy Ghost lingered
longer on Job's sorrows than it did on the
delights of Solomon, B. says, I tell Leo N.,
is he really gone, is he really in heaven now,
a heaven you yourself believe in, the
passageway into the other world, says Leo
N., is described as stepping through a
waterfall, and the vulture flies through the
sun, I went into his room, up to a bed that is
empty and say to him *I feel better today*, but

I am thinking : I NO LONGER have any hope
for this life, at 3 o'clock in the morning the
word *Arezzo* comes to mind, but really on
my mind is the fact that your best friend did
not come to your burial, I tell him, and now
giving serious consideration as to how I'll get
to the *Doctor Shop* this time, it's on Reisner
Street, been there 100 x, I tell Leo N., *early
in the morning that's when I want to die, or equinox
willowy cross*, on Saturday when there's no
mail delivered and I flee the building in utter
desperation, etc., Bataille writes, death is the
most dreadful thing that can possibly befall
us, I say to Leo N., a rush into your fantasy,
tell him, I tell Leo N., and then my saliva runs
down into what I've written what I've
sketched, because I feel the need to spit
everything out, I believe, myself and
everything, everything, I scream, my spit into
the wastepaper basket, he spit into a
wastepaper basket full of crumpled-up

paper, spit the little snot-rag into the
wastepaper basket *and then just puffed
away*, Anna sends me a little book with
black snowflakes / pearls, they run down the
page as black tears, dreamt : the ground is
rusty from red flowers, *and teased the
brewery, the tongue of sympathy*, I tell
him, and then, ACADEMY across the way
just manages to get us into the SOFITEL
Hotel vestibule and then I was so *exhausted*
by his weakness, I tell Leo N., it had passed
to me, and then I carried him on my arm in
my arms, through remembering, arcades (of
Meran) etc., possibly should be given last
rites now, he says, at the moment I began
hazily I saw *the minor condition* cafe
actually I believe I will limp *hobble into* the
beyond I believe I was looking for a different
word he says, *hoot into* eternity, in 100 years
things are going to look a lot different here,
hooted over into the beyond, etc., when did

he see St Stephen's Cathedral for the last
time, when were we last in St Stephen's
Square, SUBDATUM, *my dearest my sweet
bud of May*, etc., am utterly inconsolable, I
tell him, are you looking over my shoulder,
what am I going to eat, where shall I go to
get something to eat, dreaming : the embankment
with dry trough, dreaming : saw a cart full of
swamp green cattle, etc., on this
broken-down sofa / trundle bed, a bolster
also an arm support *cylinder with a part
down both sides of a piece of furniture*—he
lay there with nothing on, in the middle of
summer, with glowing white skin, lying
handsomely half-turned to his left side his
knees slightly bent and there through his
thighs his sex silver with sweat *heights of
dreaming*, etc., I tell Leo N., there was a
drop of raspberry juice on his finger, his
glasses had slipped off, his claw his hoof
reaching up into the air, I believe, and raised

his arm, his forehead amphora.

A long time ago a very long time ago and
everything had to be cleaned *the dog the
passer-by*, what do I know of what has come to
pass, his slight indifference corresponds to my
slight indifference, wonderful concordance, I
was *not hot today not hot enough to write*, I tell
Leo N., here raging weather, we hold to the
written word, because, we have no other
stairway, Thomas Kling writes, after our
telephone conversation I reach for 'Graves of
Honour at the Central Cemetery in Vienna' and
check to see where he is now .. the small
sapling on the terrace is *wafting or snorting*, I
tell Leo N., and Giuseppe Zigaina telephones
from Udine, and I see the black-and-white
terrier in the stairwell of this building a worker in
a dirty white uniform, down on my knees my
writing, because no room on the table, early
this morning misplaced my ears, your left eye
seems to be smaller than your right 1, says

Otto B. in a dream, yes I say an INCUBATOR,
etc., the light in my eyes has already been
almost extinguished, the flickering will soon
come to an end, the midsummer day now so
weakly lit, I say in my dream, life no longer
makes him happy but he doesn't want to die, I
say to Leo N., when he confessed to B. opened
up I ran *whilst whining* away and back home,
my own DUSTFUL END is approaching, I tell
Leo N., he dedicated a copy of a cardiogram
done a number of years ago with these words,
on the lower margin of the page, 'YOURS IS
MY HEART' and I still don't understand why he
asked for that pencil, I tell B., not able to
ask for it, was he no longer able to speak, in
your yellow garden, I say to him, as in our most
distant garden it rains golden rain blossoms, he
speaks into the hollow of his hand, a small
animal in the hollow of his hand, spoken into
the hollow of his hand, a small animal like this,
he says, a small animal like this would be nice,

to hold a small animal like this in my hand, bird,
dormouse, squirrel, as we slowly climb the
stairs, *with the snot-rag*, out to the Croatian
restaurant next door to the supermarket, he
repeats FRANCIS BACON'S DICTUM THAT
IN HIS WORK AN ARTIST MUST GIVE
CHANCE ITS RIGHTFUL PLACE WHILE
STILL STRIVING FOR THE HIGHEST
POSSIBLE LEVEL OF PRECISION, THAT'S
BEEN OUR MAXIM, TOO, HASN'T IT, it was
cobblestoned and it was somewhere in the
German Democratic Republic and we had a
meeting with Frau Oeschlegel and in the
lift at our hotel she said to me, You are the
Queen of the Night, no, I replied, I'm a morning
person, etc., oh we start to remember things we
never actually experienced, I am so
uninhabited, I say to him, I am so unused to
being with other people now that you're no
longer here, I say, when I have to spend time
with other people my heart starts racing, in the

morning when everything tastes like paper,
heavenly host sticking to my palate, then
just let it be, I tell myself, it is disaster,
depravity, blasphemy, frivolity, any attempt to
force myself to keep working, no longer go to
this restaurant, cannot go to that one either,
because we went there together so often, I say
to Leo N., there were red fingers the sprayers'
flaming bangs on the walls of the building of the
alleys we wandered through, in the '50s always
thought that *playing pinball was somewhat
obscene*, I take walks in the most beautiful
cemeteries I can find, Thomas Kling writes,
from now on there will be 1 place, 1 very
specific place. Your grave is in an outstanding
location, Thomas Kling writes. And if I am
buried face down, as I wish to be, we will lie
mouth to mouth, I write to Thomas Kling,
kissing an eternal kiss, once 1 single time fly
the Concorde, he says, 4 hours to New York, I
already know how I'll feel when the affable
pharmacist in Bad Ischl expresses his
condolences, with this HAND DIGNITY, etc.,

during a manic phase, I tell Leo N., he
proclaimed : *the world is noisy : noise is
beautiful*. 1/2 hour I will have to walk through
the forest with clover on my throat, stern-
minded, at the edge of the forest, while we
walking along the edge of the forest, we started
discussing possible titles for my next book,
I tell Leo N., while, and chewed, it was August,
the corn was already as tall as a man, and I
was walking in his shadow, what about this snot-
rag, *tongue* of spit, I say to him, on the day
after your burial bit myself in the tongue, yes,
almost bit my tongue off, blood flowing from her
mouth, and called her doctor saying she had
almost bitten her tongue off, in lots of pain, and
her doctor laughed, and she could hardly
speak, her doctor laughed, and promised to
come by, I'll send you a few cuttings I mean to
say copies of my new work, I tell my doctor,
without masquerade / make-up don't leave the
place, etc., *oh shredded signs*, *everything's
about to become fetish*, *right*, on the rim of my
glass a fruit fly, this manic tongue stuff, the

yellow feet : naked yellow sacks of a sitting
person in the bathroom, I think mouth slightly
open and protruding my rouged cheek ..
whereto gone foot and feet, like lines suddenly
broken off, right, *now what shall I do with his
clothes?*, after a fast day like this, I tell him,
there are days in slow motion, gypsied :
admittedly, on that day at noon was stuffing my
mouth full of a steaming stalk of cauliflower
gulped it down, I tell him, instead of sitting with
you, stuff my maw full of a BUNCH bushes
bouquets of cauliflower ('fits of hunger / pangs
of hunger'), I mean at midday, *at this point he
had 6 more hours to live*, and I was shovelling
this stuff into my mouth instead of helping you, I
say to him, but he doesn't hear me, he's gone
to the toilet, he can hardly stand up, he's got his
arms wrapped around B.'s neck, I tell Leo N.,
me immobile : next to him frozen, *they came to
visit me, they've been looking for me*, he says,
and falling into a chair brought in from the
ambulance, IS TIME A TENDERNESS

DRAUGHTSMAN, *and we rush away from each other or simply past one another when one of us must part from the other, into the apart.* ('like tears / he grasped my hand / these 1 thousand miles and mice ..')

August 2000

On : *ottos mops*

otto's pug

in a countermovement godlike I mean when
this sweet pug comes to the door and knocks;
identifying with this creature it seems : but
actually referring to the author's linguistic
reflections on one vowel : he is singing the
high song of O, of the O-animal, of the O-
god, ohgodohgod, of the dog owner Otto, of
the pug who found his way back home, and
we all cry and we all laugh, and our
sym-pathy, our being-touched, which finds
itself transported back to primal memories of
childhood experiences with animals, in

thus a naive one, one endowed with utter
limitlessness, a feeling, that can be attributed
both to this charming pug owner, who has lost
his pug but continues to go about his daily
business undaunted ('gets coal' and
'gets fruit') and to this sweet pug creature,
too, it's 'pugnacious' and it 'pukes'.
The more often we encounter him, in the
poem, the more certain we arc that a trans-
formation is taking place, a transformation
which succeeds, miraculously, again and
again, and that stemming from this
love for a vowel and for the reality of
the image; from a belief in this O to the
revelation poesy.

1976

ottos mops

ottos mops trotzt
otto: fort mops fort
ottos mops hopst fort
otto: soso

otto holt koks
otto holt obst
otto horcht
otto: mops mops
otto hofft

ottos mops klopft
otto: komm mops komm
ottos mops kommt
ottos mops kotzt
otto: ogottogott

Postscript

I wrote this text in 1976, we still had years
before us, in hindsight a long time. I wish we
could have one single year back of what is
for me a time I can hardly remember : how
intensively I would live it, how tenderly and
how happily.

19 July 2000

Variation on a Poem by Ernst Jandl

otto's mutts

otto's mutts mope
otto: off mutts off
otto's mutts hop off
otto: so so

otto's coals glow
otto's rose grows
otto's cold
otto: mutts mutts
otto hopes

otto's mutts roam home
otto: come mutts come
otto's mutts come
otto's mutts up chuck
otto: oh god good god